A Month with
St Augustine

Edited by Rima Devereaux

T0335271

First published in Great Britain in 2018

Society for Promoting Christian Knowledge
36 Causton Street
London SW1P 4ST
www.spck.org.uk

British Library Cataloguing-in-Publication Data
A catalogue record for this book is available from the British Library

ISBN 978-0-281-07898-1
eBook ISBN 978-0-281-07899-8

Typeset by Fakenham Prepress Solutions, Fakenham, Norfolk NR21 8NN
Manufacture managed by Jellyfish
First printed in Great Britain by CPI
Subsequently digitally printed in Great Britain

eBook by Fakenham Prepress Solutions, Fakenham, Norfolk NR21 8NN

Produced on paper from sustainable forests

Introduction

St Augustine (354–430) was born in North Africa, the son of St Monica. Despite having been brought up as a Christian, in his youth he was devoted to the pursuit of pleasure and was attracted to the Manichaean heresy, which views the world as a battleground between the forces of light and darkness. His conversion at the age of 33 in a garden in Milan marked the turning point of his life. He heard a child singing 'Take up and read', and felt that God was asking him to take up the letters of St Paul. He went on to become a priest, bishop, writer and Doctor of the Church.

Most of the extracts in this devotional are taken from the *Confessions*, which Augustine probably wrote when he was 43. His motivation for writing might have been to allay his contemporaries' suspicions of his pagan-influenced education. The book is confessional in three senses: it is an account of his sins, a statement of Christian faith and a work praising God. It contains extended prayers that encompass such movements of the heart as repentance, love and thanksgiving, and give a sense of the mystery and mercy of God.

The *Confessions* is rightly praised as a masterpiece of literature:

> The work has a perennial power to speak, even though written virtually sixteen centuries ago . . . The contemporary reader today may find much of it so 'modern' that at times it is a shock to discover how very ancient are the presuppositions and the particular context in which the author wrote.[1]

The book gives a powerful sense of salvation history: 'Like other Fathers of the Church, Augustine was vividly conscious of the entire mystery of salvation as embodied in a story that runs from Genesis to Revelation but still continues. He was himself caught up in it.'[2] Across the centuries, Augustine invites the modern reader to a fresh conversion and a rediscovery of the roots of Christian faith.

A Month with
St Augustine

DAY 1

Morning

You are great, O Lord, and greatly to be praised; your power is great, and your wisdom infinite . . . You awake us to delight in your praise; for you made us for yourself, and our heart is restless until it rests in you. Grant me, Lord, to know and understand which is first, to call on you or to praise you; and, again, to know you or to call on you. For who can call on you, not knowing you? For the one that does not know you may call on you as someone other than you are. Or is it rather that we call on you so that we may come to know you? . . . Those who seek the Lord shall praise him: for those who seek shall find him, and those who find shall praise him.

Evening

What are you then, my God? What, but the Lord God? For who is Lord but the Lord? Or who is God save our God? Most high, most good, most mighty, most powerful; most merciful, yet most just; most hidden, yet most present; most beautiful, yet most strong; stable, yet incomprehensible; unchangeable, yet all-changing; never new, never old; all-renewing and bringing age upon the proud without their knowing it; ever working, ever at rest; still gathering, yet lacking nothing; supporting, filling and overspreading; creating, nourishing and maturing; seeking, yet having all things.

DAY 2

Morning

In boyhood itself, however . . . I did not love studying, and hated being forced to it. Yet I was forced; and this was well done for me, though not by my will; for, unless forced, I would not have learnt. But no one does well unwillingly, even though what is done may be done well. Yet neither did those who forced me do well, but what was done well came to me from you, my God. For they did not consider how I should employ what they forced me to learn, except to satiate the insatiable desires of a wealthy beggary, and a shameful glory. But you, by whom the very hairs of our head are numbered, did use for my good the error of all who urged me to learn.

Evening

Yet, Lord, to you, the Creator and Governor of the universe, most excellent and most good, thanks were due to you our God, even if you had destined me for boyhood only. For even then I was, I lived, and felt; and had an implanted providence over my well-being – a trace of that mysterious Unity from which I was derived; I guarded by the inward sense the entireness of my senses, and in these small pursuits, and in my thoughts on small things, I learnt to delight in truth, I hated to be deceived, had a vigorous memory, was gifted with speech, was soothed by friendship, and avoided pain, baseness and ignorance.

DAY

3

Morning

And what was it that I delighted in, but to love and be loved? But I did not keep the measure of love, of mind to mind, friendship's bright boundary: but out of the muddy lust of the flesh and the bubblings of youth, mists fumed up which beclouded and overcast my heart, so that I could not distinguish the clear brightness of love from the fog of lustfulness . . . Your wrath had gathered over me, and I did not know it. I was grown deaf by the clanking of the chain of my mortality, the punishment of the pride of my soul, and I strayed further from you, and you let me alone, and I was tossed about, and wasted, and dissipated, and I boiled over in my fornications, and you held your peace, O you my tardy joy!

Evening

For there is an attractiveness in beautiful bodies, in gold and silver, and all things; and in bodily touch, sympathy has much influence, and each other sense has its proper object answerably tempered. Worldly honour also has its grace, and the power of overcoming, and of mastery, from which springs also the thirst of revenge. But yet, to obtain all these, we may not depart from you, O Lord, nor decline from your law. The life also which we live here has its own enchantment, through a certain proportion of its own and a correspondence with all things beautiful here below. Human friendship also is prized for the warm ties that bind many souls together in unity.

DAY

4

Morning

And so I fell among people, arrogant ranters, full of low talk, in whose mouths were the snares of the devil, limed with a mixture of the syllables of your name, and of our Lord Jesus Christ, and of the Holy Spirit, the Paraclete, our Comforter. These names departed out of their mouth as far as the sound only and the noise of the tongue, for the heart was void of truth. Yet they cried out 'Truth, Truth' and spoke much of this to me, yet it was not in them: but they spoke falsehood, not of you only (who truly are Truth), but even of those elements of this world, your creatures.

Evening

I did not know that true inward righteousness that judges not according to custom but out of the most rightful law of God almighty, whereby the standards of places and times were formed according to those times and places; the law itself meantime being the same always and everywhere, not one thing in one place, and another in another. According to this law Abraham and Isaac and Jacob and Moses and David were righteous, and all those commended by the mouth of God; but were judged unrighteous by foolish people, judging out of human judgement, and measuring by their own petty habits the moral habits of the whole human race.

DAY

5

Morning

So in acts of violence, where there is a wish to hurt, whether by reproach or injury; and these either for revenge, as one enemy against another; or for some profit belonging to another, as the robber to the traveller; or to avoid some evil, as towards one who is feared; or through envy, as one less fortunate to one more so, or one who had profited in anything, to him whose being on a par with himself he fears, or grieves at, or for the mere pleasure at another's pain, as spectators of gladiators, or deriders and mockers of others. These be the heads of iniquity which spring from the lust of the flesh, of the eye, or of rule.

Evening

And you sent your hand from above, and drew my soul out of that profound darkness, my mother, your faithful one, weeping to you for me, more than mothers weep over the bodily deaths of their children. For she, by that faith and spirit which she had from you, discerned the death wherein I lay, and you heard her, O Lord; you heard her and did not despise her tears, which, when streaming down, watered the ground under her eyes in every place where she prayed; yes, you heard her . . . O Good omnipotent, who so cares for every one of us, as if you cared for that one only; and care for all, as if they were but one!

DAY

6

Morning

In those years when I first began to teach rhetoric in my native town, I had made someone my friend, particularly dear to me from a sharing of pursuits, of my own age and, like myself, in the first opening flower of youth. He had grown up from childhood with me, and we had been both schoolmates and playmates. But he was not yet my friend as later, nor even then, as true friendship is; for true it cannot be unless in such as you cement together, cleaving to you, by that love which is shed abroad in our hearts by the Holy Spirit, which is given to us.

Evening

At this grief my heart was utterly darkened; and whatever I beheld was death. My native country was a torment to me, and my father's house a strange unhappiness; and whatever I had shared with him, wanting him, became a distracting torture. My eyes sought him everywhere, but he was not granted to them; and I hated all places because they did not have him, nor could they now tell me 'he is coming', as when he was alive and absent. I became a great riddle to myself, and I asked my soul why it was so sad and why it disquieted me so much: but it did not know what to answer me.

DAY

7

Morning

This is it that is loved in friends; and so loved that a man's conscience condemns itself if he does not love him that loves him again, or does not love again him that loves him, looking for nothing from his person but indications of his love . . . For he alone loses no one dear to him, to whom all are dear in him who cannot be lost. And who is this but our God, the God that made heaven and earth, and fills them, because by filling them he created them? You lose no one, except the one who leaves. And as for the one who leaves you, where does he go or where does he return, if not from you well pleased, to you displeased? For where does he not find your law in his own punishment? And your law is truth, and truth is you.

Evening

Turn us, O God of hosts, show us your countenance, and we shall be whole. For wherever the human soul turns itself, unless towards you, it is riveted to sorrows, yes, even though it is riveted to things beautiful. And yet they, out of you, and out of the soul, would not exist unless they were from you. They rise and set; and by rising, they begin as it were to be; they grow, that they may be perfected; and perfected, they wax old and wither; and not all grow old, but all wither. So then when they rise and tend to be, the more quickly they grow that they may be, so much the more they haste not to be. This is the law of them.

Morning

Rest in him, and you will be at rest. Where are you going on these dangerous paths? Where are you going? The good that you love is from him; but it is good and pleasant through reference to him, and justly it will be embittered, because unjustly is anything loved that is from him, if he is forsaken for it. To what end then would you go on walking these difficult and toilsome paths? There is no rest where you seek it. Seek what you are seeking, but it is not there where you seek. You seek a blessed life in the land of death; it is not there. For how can there be a blessed life where there is not life itself?

Evening

And what did it profit me that all the books I could procure of the so-called liberal arts, I, the vile slave of vile affections, read by myself and understood? And I delighted in them, but did not know whence came all that therein was true or certain. For I had my back to the light and my face to the things enlightened; whence my face, with which I discerned the things enlightened, itself was not enlightened. Whatever was written, either on rhetoric or logic, geometry, music and arithmetic, by myself without much difficulty or any instructor, I understood, you know, O Lord my God; because both quickness of understanding and acuteness in discerning is your gift: yet did I not thence sacrifice to you.

DAY

9

Morning

Let the restless, the godless, depart and flee from you; yet you see them and divide the darkness . . . For where did they flee when they fled from your presence? Or where do you not find them? But they fled, that they might not see you seeing them, and, blinded, might stumble against you (because you forsake nothing you have made); the unjust, I say, might stumble upon you, and justly be hurt, withdrawing themselves from your gentleness and stumbling at your uprightness, and falling upon their own harshness. Ignorant, in truth, that you are everywhere, whom no place encompasses! You alone are near, even to those who go far from you.

Evening

But they did not know the way, your Word, by whom you made these things that they number, and themselves who number, and the sense whereby they perceive what they number, and the understanding out of which they number; or that of your wisdom there is no number. But the Only Begotten is himself made for us wisdom and righteousness and sanctification, and was numbered among us, and paid tribute to Caesar. They did not know this way to descend to him from themselves, and by him ascend to him. They did not know this way, and deemed themselves exalted among the stars and shining; and behold, they fell upon the earth, and their foolish heart was darkened.

DAY

10

Morning

O Lord God of truth, does whoever knows these things therefore please you? Surely unhappy are those who know all these things and do not know you: but happy those who know you, though they do not know these things. And whoever knows both you and them is not the happier for them, but for you only, if, knowing you, that person glorifies you as God, and is thankful, and does not become vain in his or her imaginations. In the same way, they are better off who know how to possess a tree, and return thanks to you for the use of it, although they do not know how many cubits high it is, or how wide it spreads, than those who can measure it and count all its boughs, and neither own it nor know or love its Creator.

Evening

O God, my hope from my youth, where were you to me, and where had you gone? Had you not created me, and separated me from the beasts of the field and the fowls of the air? You had made me wiser, yet I walked in darkness and in slippery places, and sought you abroad outside myself, and did not find the God of my heart. I had come into the depths of the sea, and distrusted and despaired of ever finding truth. My mother had now come to me, resolute through piety, following me over sea and land, in all perils confiding in you . . . But to you, fountain of mercies, she poured forth more copious prayers and tears, so that you would hasten your help and enlighten my darkness.

DAY

11

Morning

I referred to the depth of the mysteries [of Scripture], and its authority appeared to me the more venerable and more worthy of religious credence, in that, while it lay open to all to read, it reserved the majesty of its mysteries within its profounder meaning, stooping to all in the great plainness of its words and lowliness of its style, yet calling forth the most intense application of such as are not light of heart; that so it might receive all in its open bosom . . . These things I thought about, and you were with me; I sighed, and you heard me; I wavered, and you guided me; I wandered through the broad way of the world, and you did not forsake me.

Evening

Perish everything, let us dismiss these empty vanities and take ourselves to the one search for truth! Life is vain, death uncertain; if it steals up on us suddenly, in what state shall we depart from here? And where shall we learn what we have neglected here? And shall we not rather suffer the punishment of this negligence? What if death itself cut off and end all care and feeling? Then must this be ascertained. But God forbid this! It is no vain and empty thing that the excellent dignity of the authority of the Christian faith has spread over the whole world. Never would such and so great things be wrought by God for us if with the death of the body the life of the soul came to an end.

DAY

12

Morning

As yet, although I believed and was firmly persuaded that you, our Lord the true God, who made not only our souls but our bodies, and not only our souls and bodies but all beings and all things, were undefilable and unalterable, and in no way liable to change, yet I did not understand, clearly and without difficulty, the cause of evil. And yet whatever it might be, I perceived it was to be sought out in such a way as should not constrain me to believe the immutable God to be mutable, lest I should become the very evil I was seeking out.

Evening

What were the pangs of my teeming heart, what groans, O my God! Yet even there were your ears open, and I did not know it; and when in silence I vehemently sought, those silent contritions of my soul were strong cries to your mercy . . . But you, Lord, abide for ever, yet not for ever are you angry with us; because you pity our dust and ashes, and it was pleasing in your sight to reform my deformities; and by inward goads you roused me so that I should be ill at ease until you were manifested to my inward sight. Thus, by the secret hand of your medicining was my swelling abated, and the troubled and bedimmed eyesight of my mind by the smarting anointings of healthful sorrows was from day to day healed.

DAY

13

Morning

O my God, let me, with thanksgiving, remember and confess to you your mercies towards me. Let my bones be bedewed with your love, and let them say to you, 'Who is like you, O Lord? You have broken my bonds in pieces; I will offer you the sacrifice of thanksgiving.' And how you have broken them, I will declare; and all who worship you, when they hear this, shall say, 'Blessed be the Lord, in heaven and in earth, great and wonderful is his name.' Your words had stuck fast in my heart, and I was hedged round about on all sides by you. Of your eternal life I was now certain, though I saw it in a figure and as through a glass.

Evening

I heard from a neighbouring house a voice, whether of a boy or a girl I do not know, chanting and frequently repeating, 'Take up and read; take up and read.' . . . I arose, interpreting it to be no other than a command from God to open the book and read the first chapter I should find . . . I seized, opened and in silence read that section on which my eyes first fell: 'Not in rioting and drunkenness, not in chambering and wantonness, not in strife and envying; but put on the Lord Jesus Christ, and make not provision for the flesh in lust.' No further would I read, nor did I need to, for instantly . . . by a light, as it were of serenity infused into my heart, all the darkness of doubt vanished away.

DAY

14

Morning

It had at first troubled me that in this very summer my lungs began to give way, amid too great literary labour, and to breathe deeply with difficulty, and by the pain in my chest to show that they were injured, and to refuse any full or lengthened speaking; this had troubled me, for it almost constrained me of necessity to lay down that burden of teaching, or, if I could be cured and recover, at least to leave it for a while. But when the full wish for leisure, that I might see how you are the Lord, arose and was fixed in me, my God, you know I began even to rejoice that I had this secondary – and real, not pretend – excuse.

Evening

Let me know you, O Lord, who know me: let me know you as I am known. Power of my soul, enter into it, and fit it for yourself, that you may have and hold it without spot or wrinkle. This is my hope, therefore I speak; and in this hope I rejoice, when I rejoice healthfully. Other things of this life are the less to be sorrowed for, the more they are sorrowed for; and the more to be sorrowed for, the less people sorrow for them. For behold, you love the truth, and whoever does likewise comes to the light. This I would do in my heart before you in confession, and in my writing, before many witnesses.

DAY

15

Morning

But what do I love, when I love you? Not beauty of bodies, nor the fair harmony of time, nor the brightness of the light, so pleasing to our eyes, nor sweet melodies of varied songs, nor the fragrant smell of flowers and ointments, and spices, not manna and honey, not limbs acceptable to the embrace of flesh. None of these I love, when I love my God; and yet I love a kind of light and melody and fragrance and meat and embrace when I love my God, the light, melody, fragrance, meat, embrace of my inner self . . . This is what I love when I love my God.

Evening

Too late I loved you, O Beauty of ancient days, yet ever new! Too late I loved you! And behold, you were within, and I abroad, and there I searched for you; I deformed, plunging amid those fair forms that you had made. You were with me, but I was not with you. Things held me far from you, which, unless they were in you, were not at all. You called and shouted and burst my deafness. You flashed, shone and scattered my blindness. You breathed fragrance, and I drew in breath and panted for you. I tasted, and I hunger and thirst. You touched me, and I burned for your peace.

DAY

16

Morning

Because now certain offices of human society make it necessary to be loved and feared by people, the adversary of our true blessedness harasses us, everywhere spreading his snares of 'well done, well done'; so that, greedily catching at them, we may be taken unawares and sever our joy from your truth, and set it in the deception of human beings; and be pleased at being loved and feared, not for your sake, but in your stead . . . But we, O Lord, behold we are your little flock; possess us as yours, stretch your wings over us, and let us fly under them. Be our glory; let us be loved for you, and your word feared in us.

Evening

Lord, since eternity is yours, are you ignorant of what I say to you? Or do you see in time what passes in time? Why then do I lay in order before you so many writings? Not, truly, that you might learn them through me, but to stir up my own and my readers' devotions towards you, that we may all say, 'Great is the Lord, and greatly to be praised.' I have said already, and again will say, for love of your love I do this. For we pray also, and yet Truth has said, 'Your Father knows what you have need of before you ask.'

DAY
17

Morning

You call us then to understand the Word, God, with you God, which is spoken eternally, and by it are all things spoken eternally. For what was spoken was not spoken successively, one thing concluded that the next might be spoken, but all things together and eternally. Otherwise we have time and change, and not a true eternity nor true immortality. This I know, O my God, and give thanks. I know, I confess to you, O Lord, and with me there know and bless you all those who are not unthankful to assure truth. We know, Lord, we know: anything that was and now is not, or is now and was not, must die and rise again. Nothing then of your Word gives place or replace, because it is truly immortal and eternal.

Evening

In this beginning, O God, you have made heaven and
earth, in your Word, in your Son, in your Power, in
your Wisdom, in your Truth; wondrously speaking
and wondrously making . . . What is that which shines
through me and strikes my heart without hurting it, and
I shudder and catch fire? . . . It is Wisdom, Wisdom's self
which shines through me . . . For my strength is brought
down in need, so that I cannot support my blessings, till
you, Lord, who have been gracious to all my iniquities,
shall heal all my infirmities. For you shall also redeem my
life from corruption, and crown me with loving kindness
and tender mercies, and shall satisfy my desire with
good things, because my youth shall be renewed like an
eagle's.

DAY

18

Morning

But because your loving-kindness is better than all lives, behold, my life is but a distraction, and your right hand upheld me, in my Lord the Son of Man, the mediator between you, the One, and us many, many also through our manifold distractions amid many things, that by him I may apprehend in whom I have been apprehended, and may be recollected from my old conversation, to follow the One, forgetting what is behind, and not distended but extended, not to things that shall be and shall pass away, but to those things that are before, not distractedly but intently, I follow on for the prize of my heavenly calling, where I may hear the voice of your praise and contemplate your delights, neither to come nor to pass away.

Evening

My heart, O Lord, touched with the words of your holy Scripture, is much busied amid this poverty of my life. And therefore most often the poverty of human understanding is copious in words, because enquiring has more to say than discovering, and demanding is longer than obtaining, and our hand that knocks has more work to do than our hand that receives. We hold the promise, who shall make it null? If God be for us, who can be against us? Ask, and you shall have; seek, and you shall find; knock, and it shall be opened to you. For everyone who asks, receives; and they who seek, find; and to them that knock, it shall be opened. These are your own promises: and who need fear to be deceived when the Truth promises?

DAY

19

Morning

That heaven of heavens was for yourself, O Lord; but the earth which you gave to the human race, to be seen and felt, was not such as we now see and feel. For it was invisible, without form, and there was a deep, upon which there was no light; or, darkness was above the deep, that is, more than in the deep. Because this deep of waters, visible now, has even in its depths a light proper for its nature, perceivable in whatever degree to the fishes and creeping things in the bottom of it. But that whole deep was almost nothing, because hitherto it was altogether without form; yet there was already that which could be formed.

Evening

O let the Light, the Truth, the Light of my heart, not my own darkness, speak to me. I fell off into that, and became darkened; but even then, even then I loved you. I went astray, and remembered you. I heard your voice behind me, calling to me to return, though scarcely heard it through the tumultuousness of the enemies of peace. And now, behold, I am returning in distress and panting for your fountain. Let no one forbid me! Of this will I drink and so live. Let me not be my own life; from myself I lived badly; I was death to myself, and I revive in you. Speak to me, converse with me. I have believed your books, and their words are full of mystery.

DAY

20

Morning

For although we find no time before it – for wisdom was created before all things – this is not that Wisdom which is altogether equal and coeternal with you, our God, his Father, and by whom all things were created, and in whom, as the beginning, you created heaven and earth. But it is that wisdom which is created, that is, the intellectual nature, which, by contemplating the light, is light. For this, though created, is also called wisdom. But what difference there is between the Light which enlightens and that which is enlightened, as much as there is between the Wisdom that creates and that which is created; as between the Righteousness which justifies and the righteousness which is made by justification.

Evening

For it is true, O Lord, that you made heaven and earth; and it is true too that the Beginning is your Wisdom, in which you create all: and true again that this visible world has for its greater part heaven and earth, which briefly comprise all made and created natures. And true too that whatever is mutable gives us to understand a certain want of form, whereby it receives a form, or is changed, or turned.

DAY

21

Morning

I call upon you, O my God, my mercy, who created me and did not forget me, though I forgot you. I call you into my soul, which, by the longing you yourself inspire in it, you prepare for yourself. Forsake me not now calling upon you, me whom you answered before I called, and urged me with much variety of repeated calls, that I would hear you from afar and be converted, and call upon you who called after me. For you, Lord, blotted out all my evil deserts, so as not to repay into my hands that for which I fell from you; and you have anticipated all my good deserts, so as to repay the work of your hands, the hands that made me; because before I was, you were.

Evening

Lo, now the Trinity appears to me in a glass darkly, which is you, my God, because you, O Father, in him who is the beginning of our wisdom, which is your Wisdom, born of yourself, equal to you and coeternal, that is, in your Son, created heaven and earth. Much now have we said of the heaven of heavens, and of the earth invisible and without form, and of the darksome deep, in reference to the wandering instability of its spiritual deformity, unless converted to him, from whom it had its then degree of life, and by his enlightening became a beauteous life, and the heaven of that heaven, which was afterwards set between water and water.

DAY

22

Morning

Let us look, O Lord, upon the heavens, the work of your fingers; clear from our eyes that cloud, which you have spread under them. There is your testimony, which gives wisdom to the little ones: perfect, O my God, your praise out of the mouth of babes and sucklings. For we know no other books which so destroy pride, which so destroy the enemy and the defender, who resists your reconciliation by defending his own sins. I do not know, Lord, I do not know any other such pure words, which so persuade me to confess, and bend my neck to your yoke, and invite me to serve you for nought. Let me understand them, good Father. Grant this to me, who am placed under them, because you have established these things for those placed under them.

Evening

O Lord God, give peace to us (for you have given us all things): the peace of rest, the peace of the Sabbath, which has no evening. For all this most goodly array of things very good, having finished their courses, is to pass away, for in them there was morning and evening.

But the seventh day has no evening, nor has it setting, because you have sanctified it to continue for ever. After all your works, which were very good, you rested on the seventh day, although you made them in unbroken rest, so that the voice of your Book may announce beforehand to us that we also, after our works (also very good because you have given them to us), shall rest in you in the Sabbath of eternal life.

DAY

23

Morning

How different are my days from the days of the Lord! They are 'my' days because I took them for myself, intoxicated as I was with my reckless independence which led me to abandon him; but since he is everywhere, all powerful and ever present, I fully deserved to be imprisoned in the darkness of ignorance and to bear on my feet the chains of mortality. In these days of mine I cried aloud: 'Free my soul from prison.' And he brought me help – his day of salvation. He heard the prisoner in chains in his misery and came to him. In those days of mine that are past, the sorrows of death surrounded me . . . they would not have come close to me had I not strayed so far away from you.

Evening

The Lord is merciful and just: our God gives us his mercy. He is merciful, he is just and works mercy. He has been merciful above all because he has inclined his ear to me; and I would not have known that he heard me if I had not first heard the voice of his apostles inviting me to cry out to him in my turn. No one has ever called upon him without first having been called by him. That is why he is called merciful. He is just because he metes out punishment, and he is merciful because he draws us to himself.

DAY

24

Morning

O Lord my God, if I am complaining in the midst of these people, among Christ's family, among your poor, it is because I want to be able to satisfy with your bread those people who do not hunger and thirst for righteousness but who are satiated and have plenty. Yet they are full of their own imaginings and not filled with the truth that they spurn and run away from, only to fall into their own vanity. I know from experience what deceits are generated by the human heart: and what is my heart if not a human one? . . . God is eternal truth, eternal love; love is true, eternity is true; truth is loved, as is eternity.

Evening

O Lord my God, my only hope, hear me in your goodness: grant that I may not stop seeking you when I am weary, but seek your presence ever more fervently. Give me the strength to seek you: you allow yourself to be found and inspire in me the hope of finding you through an ever-increasing knowledge of you. I lay before you my strength and my weakness: preserve my strength and heal my weakness. I lay before you my learning and my ignorance; where you open a door for me, welcome me as I go in, and where one is closed, open it to me when I knock. Let me always remember you, understand you and love you. Increase your gifts in me until in the end you transform me into a new creation.

DAY

25

Morning

O Lord our God, we believe in you, Father, Son and Holy Spirit. For the Word would not have said: 'Go, baptize all nations in the name of the Father and of the Son and of the Holy Spirit', if you were not Trinity. And you would not have commanded us to be baptized in the name of someone who was not the Lord God; nor would a voice from heaven have said: 'Hear, O Israel: the Lord your God is the only God', if you were not Trinity in being, the one Lord, the one God. And if you were God the Father and, at the same time, the Son your Word, Jesus Christ, and if you were your gift, the Holy Spirit, we would not read in holy Scripture: 'God sent his Son.'

Evening

Set me free, O God, from the abundance of words from which I suffer deep within my soul, which is unhappy in your sight and takes refuge in your mercy. Indeed, even when my lips are silent my thoughts are not. If I could at least think of something pleasing to you, then I certainly would not beg you to set me free from this surfeit of words. But my thoughts are many, and you know that human thoughts are vain. Help me not to give in to them and if ever they delight me grant that I may disapprove of them and do not abandon me to them as if to a kind of sleep.

DAY

26

Morning

I thank you, O my light, that you have lit my way and I have known you. How have I known you? I have known you as the only true and living God, my creator. I have known you as the creator of heaven and earth and of all things seen and unseen, almighty God, true, immortal, invisible, unmeasured and unbounded, eternal and inaccessible; incomprehensible, immense and infinite; the beginning of all creatures, seen and unseen, by whom all the elements are created and sustained . . . I have known you as the one unique, true and eternal God: Father, Son and Holy Spirit, three Persons but one single essence, one indivisible nature of perfect simplicity.

Evening

Give me, O Lord, a heart that thinks on you; a soul that delights in you, a mind that contemplates you, an intellect that understands you, and a reason that always remains faithful to you, most sweet one, and loves you wisely, O most wise love.

O life through whom all things live, you give me life and you are my life, life through whom I live, and without whom I die; life through whom I am brought back to life and without whom I am lost, life in whom I am lost, life in whom I rejoice, and without whom I am in torment; sweet, lovely, life-giving life who can never be forgotten.

DAY

27

Morning

O God, Creator of the universe, grant that I may learn to pray; grant that I may become worthy of being heard by you; grant that I may in the end be set free by you, God, through whom all things that would not exist on their own come into being . . . God, who has given pure hearts the gift of knowing the one true God; O God, Father of truth, Father of wisdom, Father of true life, Father of joy, Father of goodness and beauty, Father of incomprehensible light, O Father, source of our awakening and of our enlightenment, who has made a pledge with us, it is you who counsels us to return to you.

Evening

I call on you, O God our Truth, who are the source, beginning and creator of truth and of all that is true; O God our Wisdom, the source, beginning and creator of wisdom, and of all that is wise; God who are the true and sovereign Life, the source, beginning and creator of life and of all that lives in truth and sovereignty; O God our Blessedness, the source, beginning and creator of joy and of all that is joyful; God of goodness and beauty who is in all that is good and beautiful . . . God from whom to stray is to fall, and to whom to return is to rise up, in whom to remain is to rest on a firm foundation.

DAY

28

Morning

By your grace, O God, we do not suffer total death. You warn us to be watchful. By your grace we distinguish good from evil, we can shun evil and seek good and not fall into adversity. By your grace we are enabled both to command and obey. By your grace we discover that sometimes what we think is ours is alien to us and what we think is alien is ours. By your grace we are freed from the snares and attacks of evil. It is through you that little things do not make us small. By you the best in us is not suffocated by the worst in us.

Evening

You are everything, you are as much as I have said in my prayer. Come to my help, one true and eternal substance; in you there is no discord, no confusion, no change, no defect, no death; in you there reigns total harmony, total clarity and constancy, total fullness and life; in you there is neither too little nor too much; with you he who created and he who was begotten are one and the same. All things serve you and every good soul is obedient to you. Your laws govern the movement of the earth and fix the course of the stars: they give the heat of the sun by day and the gentle light of the moon by night.

DAY
29

Morning

Now it is you alone that I love, you alone that I follow, you alone that I seek, you alone that I feel ready to serve, because you alone rule justly. It is to your authority alone that I want to submit. Command me, I pray, to do whatever you will, but heal and open my ears that I may hear your voice. Heal and open my eyes that I may see your will. Drive out from me all fickleness, that I might acknowledge you alone. Tell me where to look that I may see you, and I will place my hope in doing your will. I beg you, make your son, a fugitive, welcome, O God who are more loving than any father.

Evening

I have turned back to you and ask you to give me the means to draw close to you. If you leave us we die! But you will not leave us because you are wholly good and do not let a sincere heart seek you without finding you . . . So I entrust this body of mine to you, good and wise Father . . . I want only to invoke your mighty love that I might turn wholly to you, and let nothing hold me back from drawing near to you. Let me lead a life of moderation, courage, justice and prudence, that I may love and fully understand your wisdom; make me worthy of your house, that I might become an inhabitant of your kingdom, which is the very height of happiness.

DAY

30

Morning

Hear me, my Creator, I am your creature and I am lost; I am your creature and I am dying, your creature and reduced to nothing. Your hands, O Lord, made me and formed me, those hands pierced with nails for me. Do not despise, O Lord, the work of your hands . . . Forgive me, O God, for my days have no meaning. I am ill and call for healing. I am blind and hasten towards the light. I am dead and long for life. You are healer, light and life. Jesus of Nazareth, have pity on me. Son of David, have pity on me.

Evening

O Lord, the Word, O God, the Word, you are the light and through you light was made; you are the Way, the Truth and the Life, and in you there is no darkness nor error, vanity nor death; light, without whom there is only darkness, way, aside from whom there is only error, truth, without whom there is only vanity, life, without whom there is only death, speak a word, say, O Lord, 'Let there be light', that I may see the light and avoid darkness, see the way and avoid false steps, see truth and avoid vanity, see life and avoid death.

DAY
31

Morning

Like a stag panting for the stream, so my soul longs for you, O God. My soul is thirsty for the living God. When shall I come to see the face of my God? . . . O greatest joy, joy that is above all joys, when shall I share in you and see my Lord who dwells in you? We await the Saviour, the Lord Jesus Christ, who will transform our lowly bodies so that they will be like his glorious body. We await the Lord's return from the wedding so that he may lead us in peace to his own marriage feast. Come, Lord Jesus, do not delay. Come, Lord Jesus, draw near to us in peace; come, our Saviour, come, desire of all peoples. Show us your face and we shall be saved.

Evening

O three coequal and coeternal Persons, true and living
God, Father, Son and Holy Spirit, who alone dwell in
eternity in the light that is hidden from us, who created
the earth by your power and rule the whole universe
with your wisdom, holy, holy, holy God of Sabbaoth, you
are just and merciful, wonderful, lovely and worthy of all
praise; only God, three Persons in one single essence:
power, wisdom and goodness, one and indivisible Trinity,
open the door of righteousness when I knock; when I
enter I will praise the Lord . . . let me come close to you,
O Lord my God, to see the richness of your kingdom and
your face ever before me.

Notes and sources

Notes

1   Henry Chadwick, 'Introduction', in Saint Augustine, *The Confessions*, translated by Henry Chadwick, Oxford World's Classics (New York: Oxford University Press, 1991), p. ix.
2   Maria Boulding, 'Introduction', in Saint Augustine, *The Confessions*, translated by Maria Boulding (New York: New City Press, 1997).

Sources

The Confessions of Saint Augustine, translated by Edward B. Pusey (London: J. M. Dent & Sons, 1907). The text has been lightly modernized by Hannah Ward and Jennifer Wild.

Praying with Augustine, compiled by Valeria Boldoni, translated by Paula Clifford (London: Triangle/SPCK, 1997) – for prayers taken from works other than the *Confessions*.

The texts have been lightly modernized by Hannah Ward and Jennifer Wild.

Confessions
Day 1: Morning, 1.1; Evening, 1.4
Day 2: Morning, 1.12; Evening, 1.20
Day 3: Morning, 2.2; Evening, 2.5
Day 4: Morning, 3.6; Evening, 3.7
Day 5: Morning, 3.8; Evening, 3.11
Day 6: Morning, 4.4; Evening, 4.4
Day 7: Morning, 4.9; Evening, 4.10
Day 8: Morning, 4.12; Evening, 4.16
Day 9: Morning, 5.2; Evening, 5.3
Day 10: Morning, 5.4; Evening, 6.1
Day 11: Morning, 6.5; Evening, 6.11
Day 12: Morning, 7.3; Evening, 7.7–8
Day 13: Morning, 8.1; Evening, 8.12
Day 14: Morning, 9.2; Evening, 10.1
Day 15: Morning, 10.6; Evening, 10.27
Day 16: Morning, 10.36; Evening, 11.1
Day 17: Morning, 11.7; Evening, 11.9
Day 18: Morning, 11.29; Evening, 12.1
Day 19: Morning, 12.8; Evening, 12.10
Day 20: Morning, 12.15; Evening, 12.19
Day 21: Morning, 13.1; Evening, 13.5
Day 22: Morning, 13.15; Evening, 13.35–6

Commentary on the Psalms
Day 23: Morning, 116.3

On the Trinity
Day 24: Morning, 4, Proemio; Evening, 15.28
Day 25: Morning, 15.28; Evening, 15.28

Soliloquies
Day 26: Evening, 1
Day 27: Morning, 1.2; Evening, 1.3a
Day 28: Morning, 1.3b; Evening, 1.4
Day 29: Morning, 1.5; Evening, 1.6
Day 30: Morning, 2; Evening, 4
Day 31: Morning, 35; Evening, 37